MIKE THALER PRESENTS...

PROPHETS OF THE BIBLE
GOD'S ANCHORMEN
5 FUN BIBLE STORIES

BY MIKE THALER
ILLUSTRATIONS BY DENNIS ADLER

Equipping Kids for Life!
faithkids.com

A Faith Building Guide can be found on page 32.

Dedicated to
Greg Johnson
alive for God.
Mike

Faith Kids® is an imprint of
Cook Communications, Colorado Springs, Colorado 80918
Cook Communications, Paris, Ontario
Kingsway Communications, Eastbourne, England

PROPHETS OF THE BIBLE
© 2002 by Mike Thaler for text and Dennis Adler for illustrations

All rights reserved. Except for brief excerpts for review purposes,
no part of this book may be reproduced or used in any form
without written permission from the publisher.

Faith Kids® is a registered trademark of Cook Communications Ministries.

Published in association with the literary agency of Alive Communications, Inc.,
7680 Goddard St., Suite 200, Colorado Springs CO 80920.

Edited by Heather Gemmen
Designed by Clyde Van Cleve

First printing, 2002
Printed in Singapore
06 05 04 03 02   5 4 3 2 1

Library of Congress Cataloging-in-Publication Data

Thaler, Mike, 1936-
  Prophets of the Bible : God's anchormen / by Mike Thaler ; illustrated by Dennis Adler.
    p. cm. --
  Summary: Five comical retellings of stories of Biblical prophets: Elisha, Samuel, Ezra,
Ezekiel, and Jeremiah, showing what happened when they listened to God.
  ISBN 0-7814-3650-
  1. Bible stories, English--O.T.--Juvenile humor. [1. Bible stories--O.T. 2.
Bible O.T.--Wit and humor.] I. Adler, Dennis (Dennis H.), 1942- ill. II. Title.

BS551.3 .T475 2002
221.9'505--dc21
                                                                    2001055680

"Mike Thaler is proof positive that the funny bone is connected to the learning bone."

— Emmett Cooper, Ph.D
President, HoneyWord® Way of Learning

Mike Thaler Presents . . .

- Action Heroes of the Bible: The Sermonators
- Prophets of the Bible: God's Anchormen
- Heroines of the Bible: God's Fair Ladies

Books in the Heaven and Mirth® Series:

- Adam and the Apple Turnover
- Moses: Take Two Tablets and Call Me in the Morning
- The Prodigal Son: Oh Brother
- Daniel: Nice Kitty!
- David & Bubblebath Sheba
- David: God's Rock Star
- Elijah: Prophet Sharing
- John the Baptist, Wet & Wild
- Paul: God's Message Sent Apostle Post

"A romping fun read-aloud for kids (and grown-ups who still like to grin)."

— Becky Freeman
Best-selling author and speaker

"Out loud! Out loud! This book must be read out loud! Why? Because that's the way that kids will laugh—OUT LOUD! That's the way that parents will laugh! And everyone will learn because laughter lubricates learning."

— Calvin Miller
Best-selling author and speaker

Elisha*
The Man Who Came to Dinner

ELIJAH'S GOLDEN CHARIOT swirled up to heaven in a whirlwind. "Drop your coat and the car keys!" shouted Elisha. When Elijah heard that, he knew Elisha was a true prophet because cars hadn't been invented yet. So he dropped Elisha his coat and Elisha became his successor.

* pronounced *a-leash-a*

Now Elisha was a pretty good prophet.
But as a beginner he made a few mistakes.
He didn't buy IBM® stock at 7.
He voted for Thomas E. Dewey.
And he predicted that Elvis
had no future in the music business.
But all in all he was pretty cool.
He was especially successful with oil
and water—and he was on the road a lot
helping people make salad dressing
and teaching them about God.

One day he was passing through
a little town called Shunen*
and a nice lady named Mrs. Johnson
invited him to stay for dinner.

"What are you having?" asked Elisha.
"Just kidding. Sure I'll stay."

The dinner was so good
Elisha stayed for breakfast, lunch,
and dinner the next day.
In fact he stayed for so many meals
that the lady built another room
onto her house for him.
Then he stayed a lot more—
and gained a lot of weight.

* a town not many people visited

He was so grateful that one day
he asked Mrs. Johnson
what he could do to help her.

"Well, to start off,
don't leave your sandals
around the living room."

"Okay," said Elisha. "Anything else?"

"You could blow out the lamp
when you're not in your room."

"Anything else?"

"You could help with the dishes sometimes."

"Okay, anything else?"

"No, that about does it."

"How about a magazine subscription,
or a new welcome mat, or a son?"

"A son would be nice," said the lady.

"Okay," said Elisha.
"Next year at this time you'll have one."

And sure enough she did.
He was a cute little kid,
and she called him Howard.

But one day when she and Howard
were out in the field working,
Howard grabbed his head
and yelled,
"My head! My head!"

"What about your head?"
asked Mrs. Johnson.

But Howard didn't answer—
he was dead.
Mrs. Johnson
jumped on her donkey,
and rode as fast as she could to Elisha.
Being a smart prophet he asked,
"What's the matter?"

"It's Howard!" she shouted.

"What's wrong?"

"Only one thing."

"What's that?"

"He's dead!"

So Elisha jumped on her donkey
and they both rode back to the field
where Howard was lying.
Elisha leapt off and gave him
eye-to-eye resuscitation.

Howard opened his eyes and said,
"Boy, do I have a headache."

Everyone rejoiced
and they all went in
and had lunch.

P.S. When he grew up,
Howard and his mom,
Mrs. Johnson,
opened rooms for travelers
all over the land.
They called them motels.
Elisha thought they'd never be successful—
but nobody's perfect.

The End

Nuggets from Goldie, the miner prophet:
"If you give a prophet a muffin, he may move in."

For the real story, read 2 Kings 4:8–37.

Elisha Floating Alone

ALL THE PROPHETS decided to build a new clubhouse. "This one's too small," they told Elisha. "And we don't have indoor plumbing."

"Go," said Elisha.

"Won't you come and help?" they all asked.

Now Elisha was not
into manual labor—
he was more of an
idea man.
   But he said, "Sure."

So they all headed
for the Jordan
and started
chopping down trees.
In the middle of a swing,
one prophet's ax head
got angry and flew off the handle.
It landed splash in the middle
of the river and sank—
blub, blub, blub.

"Hey," said the prophet.
"That's rented equipment,
and I have to get
my deposit back."

"No problem," smiled Elisha,
walking to the river bank,
and he threw in the handle too.
It floated,
   and to everyone's amazement,
   so did the ax head.

The surprised prophet reached in and fished them both out.

"How do you make an ax head float?" asked the prophet.

"It's easy," said Elisha.

"Get two scoops of vanilla ice cream, root beer, and an ax head."

"Wow," said the prophet.

"That's nothing," smiled Elisha, "when I was in the Rose Parade, I made a truck float."

The End

Nuggets from Goldie, the miner prophet:
"If you lose your head, God can always help you get it back."

For the real story, read 2 Kings 6:1–7.

Samuel
A Kid with a Calling

THERE WAS A MAN NAMED ELKANAH.
He had two wives. One of them,
Peninnah, had lots of kids.
The other Hannah had none.
Peninnah teased Hannah every day.
She'd say things like:
"It's inconceivable
that you can't have kids,"
or, "You better call
womb service."
Peninnah egged her on
at every opportunity.

So Hannah cried out to God,
and God heard her.
He gave her a son,
whom she named Samuel.

In gratitude, she sent him to Hebrew school
when he was only six months old.
He learned fast and was bar mitzvahed
at thirteen months, after which
he helped Eli, the head priest,
do chores around the temple.

Now Eli had two sons, Hophni
and Phinehas. They didn't help their
dad at all. In fact, they were downright
wicked. They made hero sandwiches
out of temple sacrifices, they kissed girls,
and they made jokes during the services.
Finally God got fed up with the whole family
and decided to send Eli a telegram, saying,
"You're fired!"

That night God called to Samuel, **"Hey, Samuel!"**

Samuel got up and went to Eli. "What is it?"

"Go back to bed, I didn't call you."

Samuel went back to bed.

Then God called to Samuel again, **"Hey, Samuel!"**

Samuel got up again and went to Eli. "What is it?"

"I didn't call you. Knock it off and go to bed."

Samuel went back to bed, and God called to him a third time.

Samuel got up and went to Eli again.

"Look, Samuel, I didn't call you. It must be God.
The next time He calls, if it's not collect, say,
'Speak to me, Lord. Your servant is listening.'"

Samuel did, and the Lord said, "**Samuel, you're a hard guy to get a hold of. Listen, I'm fed up! Eli and the boys have had it.**"

Samuel went back to sleep,
but in the morning Eli asked,
"Well, what did God say?
What was so important
he had to call in the middle
of the night and wake us all up?"

"He said that you and the boys
have had it."

"Well," sighed Eli.
"That's how the big bagel bounces."

After that, the Lord called Samuel a lot,
and word got out that he was a primo prophet.

Now, the Israelites got in a big fight
with the Philistines, and the Philistines beat them heartily.
After the battle, the elders of Israel asked, "What happened?
Where was the Lord? We need a little Ark support!"

17

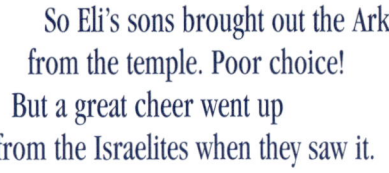

So Eli's sons brought out the Ark
from the temple. Poor choice!
But a great cheer went up
from the Israelites when they saw it.

The Philistines heard the cheering
and asked, "What are they cheering
about? We beat them today!" But then
they heard that the Ark had arrived,
and they got scared.
"Their God is with them.
He's our *Ark* enemy,
'cause He's one
mighty tough God."

So they all took out
their rabbits' feet
and rubbed them
the rest of the night.
And in the morning
they beat the Israelites again,
captured the Ark,
and bumped off Eli's boys.

A messenger ran back to town
to break the news.
He found Eli sitting in a chair
by the side of the road.

"How'd it go today?" asked Eli.

"Not bad, boss, but this Friday night's service won't be so great."

"Why's that?" asked Eli.

"Well, the Ark of the Covenant won't be there."

"Why not?" asked Eli.

"Well . . . the Philistines have it."

"How'd they get it?" asked Eli leaning forward.

"They captured it."

"How'd they capture it?" asked Eli leaning backward.

"They killed your sons, and took it."

"How'd they kill my sons?" asked Eli, rocking.

"When they wiped out our entire army."

When Eli heard this, he got so upset, he fell off his chair, and died.

Now, for the Philistines,
capturing the Ark was a mixed blessing.
They were proud to have it,
but wherever they put it,
everyone died.
They finally decided
to send it back to the Israelites.

"How should we send it?"
asked their elders.
"Fed Ex®? UPS®?
A cart with two oxen?"

"That sounds good,"
everyone agreed.
So they got a cart
with two oxen,
and sent it back.

The Israelites
were glad to see it.
But seventy of them died
just looking at it.

"Maybe we should see who else wants it,"
they whispered covering their eyes.

Samuel said, "None of you are fit to have the Ark.
You have all sinned against the Lord.

Throw away your crystals,
burn your tarot cards,
and meet me at Mizpah.
We'll ask the Lord for forgiveness."

When the Philistines heard that the Israelites
had all gathered at Mizpah,
they sharpened their swords
and marched to kill them.
But when they drew close,
the Lord thundered down at them, **"Beat it!"**
All the frightened Philistines ran away.

"See how good it is,
when you praise the Lord," said Samuel.

And as long as Samuel lived,
he and all Israel praised the Lord,
and things were very good indeed.

The End

Nuggets from Goldie, the miner prophet:
"The only safe side to be on is God's good side."

For the real story, read 1 Samuel 1–7.

Ezra
The Lord's Legal Eagle

EZRA HAD A LAW DEGREE from Bible college. He had the word on the Word. So God asked him to go to Jerusalem and straighten out the Jews. They had messed up again. They had married a lot of non-Jewish girls. They had hooked up with *Chikites*, *Girlites*, *Chipites*, and *Dollites*. They were drinkin' *Bud Lights*® and smokin' *Camelites*.

Ezra was afraid that God would lose His patience with all their philandering and finish them off—once and for all.

So he decided to go to Jerusalem and
set things right.

He had a letter
 from King Artytaxes*
 that proclaimed:

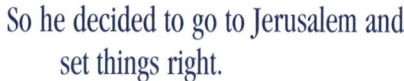

> *Listen to this guy.*
> *He knows*
> *from whence he speaks.*
> *He be cool,*
> *No fool*
> *A tool of God.*
> *So obey*
> *What he say*
> *Or pay*
> *The consequences.*

When he got to Jerusalem
things were really out of hand.
It was a lot worse
than Ezra had imagined.
Almost everyone had married *Babeites*
and was eating bowls of pork stroganoff.
Ezra tore off his clothes
and yanked out his hair.
This got their attention.

*pronounced Arty-Taxes

Then he told them God was miffed
and they had a real need, to take heed,
with speed, or lose their seed—forever.

All the Israelites fell to their knees.
"We hear you Brother Ezra, what should we do?"

"Well, first of all dump the *Fluffites*.
Then clean up your houses and your acts.
I have printed for you up a book
to relearn the laws of God:
$12.95 hard cover and $3.25 paperback.
Get it now, take it home, read it,
and do what it says.
And—by the way—pray."

So everyone bought the book,
and Ezra had to have a second printing.
Hollywood even showed some interest.
The Jews cleaned up their act,
and God forgave everyone.
Amen!

The End

Nuggets from Goldie, the miner prophet:
"If you make a bad choice, you're not hearing God's voice."

For the real story, read Ezra 7:11–10:17.

Jeremiah
Womb Service

G OD MADE A PRENATAL CALL
on Jeremiah.
**"Jeremiah, are you up?
Listen, I have chosen you
to be a prophet."**

"Lord," said Jeremiah,
"I'm just an embryo.
This is a very early career choice."

"It's never too early to start planning your future."

"But God, I haven't been born yet!"

"Grow up, Jeremiah. I've chosen you to take my word to the nations."

"But God, I can't even talk yet."

"Don't sweat it," said God putting his hand on Jeremiah's lips. **"I'll do all the talking."**

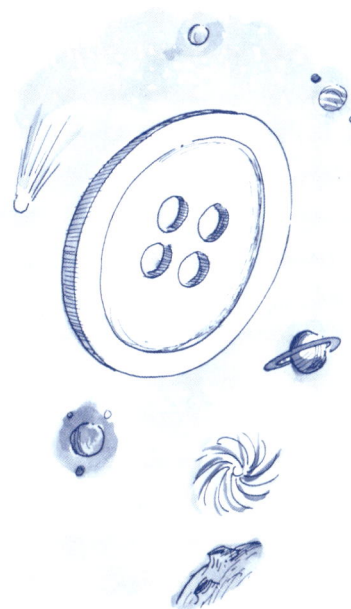

"If you say so, God."

"I do, and I have appointed and anointed you over nations and kingdoms to uproot, tear down, destroy, and overthrow— which is normal toddler behavior."

"Sounds like fun," said Jeremiah.

"Jeremiah, what do you see?"

"The inside of a belly button?"

"No, no. Over here."

"It looks a lot like the branch of an almond tree."

"Right, now what do you see?"

"I see a boiling pot tilting south."

"You're a smart embryo. Tell the folks in Jerusalem that I am going to boil their biscuits and fry their fritters."

"But, Lord, they may get angry."

"Don't worry. I'll be there with you and I will bring you strength."

"That's great, Lord. And by the way,

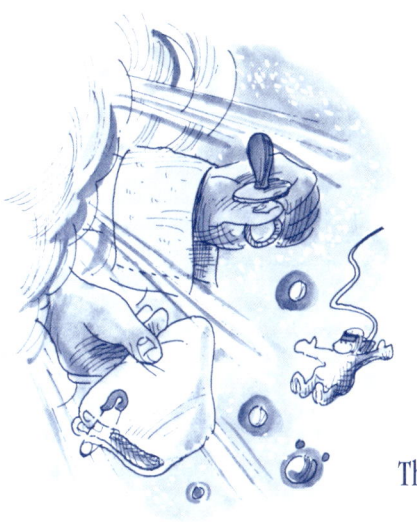

could You also bring
my binky,
my blanky,
and a clean diaper?"

The End

Nuggets from Goldie, the miner prophet:
"You're never too young to serve the Lord."

For the real story read Jeremiah 1.

MIKE THALER PRESENTS...

Life Issue: Sometimes it's hard to believe that God's idea is best.
Spiritual Building Block: Faith

Learn how to believe that God's plan is the right one for you:

Think About It:
God is pretty smart. He made everything and thought about every detail to make it run just right. He knew that when we get scratched, our body has to be able to send a message to our head to say that it hurts so we can take care of it. He knew that Earth needs to move around the sun to make seasons. He knew that fish need scales and birds need feathers. He's definitely smart. He knows what he's doing.

Talk About It:
Find a friend who has a great imagination; spend an hour or so telling each other creative stories. See how wild you can get. Now think about your stories: no matter how crazy some of your ideas were, they all grew from things in this world that you know. They were ideas that came from God's ideas. Isn't it amazing how creative and fun and interesting and beautiful God's mind is?

Try It:
God made you a wonderful person. He knows exactly what is best for you. He made you and the world you live in. Best of all, he loves you so much and wants only the best for you—even if it doesn't seem that way to you. If you know that God wants you to do something or not do something, obey him. If it's his plan, it's a good one.